Grassland Animals

Siân Smith

raintree

a Capstone company — publishers for children

Raintree is an imprint of Capstone Global Library Limited, a company incorporated in England and Wales having its registered office at 7 Pilgrim Street, London, EC4V 6LB – Registered company number: 6695582

www.raintreepublishers.co.uk
myorders@raintreepublishers.co.uk

Text © Capstone Global Library Limited 2015
First published in hardback in 2014
Paperback edition first published in 2015
The moral rights of the proprietor have been asserted.

Edited by Sian Smith and Diyan Leake
Designed by Marcus Bell
Picture research by Tracy Cummins
Production by Helen McCreath
Originated by Capstone Global Library Ltd
Printed and bound in China

ISBN 978 1 406 28066 1 (hardback)
18 17 16 15 14
10 9 8 7 6 5 4 3 2 1

ISBN 978 1 406 28073 9 (paperback)
19 18 17 16 15
10 9 8 7 6 5 4 3 2 1

British Library Cataloguing in Publication Data
Smith, Sian.
Grassland animals. -- (Animal in their habitats)
A full catalogue record for this book is available from the British Library.

Acknowledgements
We would like to thank the following for permission to reproduce photographs: Getty Images pp. 8, 22b (Beverly Joubert), Shutterstock pp. 4 (John Lindsay-Smith), 5 (john michael evan potter), 6 (Karel Gallas), 7 (KA Photography KEVM111), 9 (Cristian Zamfir), 10 (dlodewijks), 11 (Maggy Meyer), 12 (Bryan Busovicki), 13 (mj007), 14 (mariait), 15 (Christian Vinces), 16 (Pressmaster), 17 (Birdiegal), 18 (Stu Porter), 19 (James Coleman), 20a (Lukasz Janyst), 20b (szefei), 20c (Galyna Andrushko), 20d (2009fotofriends), 21 (Paul Banton), 22a (dlodewijks).

Cover photograph of giraffes crossing a stream in the Serengeti reproduced with permission of Shutterstock (Bjorn Hoglund).

Back cover photograph reproduced with permission of Shutterstock (Maggy Meyer).

We would like to thank Michael Bright for his invaluable help in the preparation of this book.

Every effort has been made to contact copyright holders of material reproduced in this book. Any omissions will be rectified in subsequent printings if notice is given to the publisher.

Contents

Animals that live on grasslands

zebra

Here is a zebra.

Here is an elephant.

Here is a giraffe.

Here is a rhino.

Here is a baboon.

Here is an ostrich.

Here is a gazelle.

Here is a lion.

Here is a cheetah.

Here is a buffalo.

Here is a horse.

Here is an owl.

Here is a rabbit.

Here is a fox.

Here is a serval.

Here is a skunk.

All about grasslands

Grasslands are really big pieces of land covered in grass. There are grasslands all over the world.

Can you spot the grassland?

Answer: d

What am I?

I have four legs.

I eat grass.

I am a member of the horse family.

I have stripes.

Picture glossary

 **baboon**

 **gazelle**

Index

Notes for teachers and parents

Before reading

Tuning in: Talk about why lots of animals live in grasslands. Why might it be a good place for them to live?

After reading

Recall and reflection: Which is the tallest grassland animal? (giraffe) Which grassland animal runs the fastest? (cheetah)

Sentence knowledge: Help the child to count the number of words in each sentence.

Word knowledge (phonics): Challenge the child to find an animal beginning with *z* on p. 4 and an animal beginning with *e* on p. 5.

Word recognition: Challenge the child to race you to point at the word *is* on any page.

Rounding off

Sing the following song (to the tune of "John Brown's Body"):
In the sunny grasslands you can see five elephants (3 times)
And they eat and eat and eat all day.
(Continue with: *four tall giraffes that stride, three buffalo that graze, two swift gazelles that run, hear a hooting owl that flaps all night*)

Word coverage

Topic words
baboon
buffalo
cheetah
elephant
fox
gazelle
giraffe
grassland
horse
lion
ostrich
owl
rabbit
rhino
serval
skunk
zebra

High-frequency words
a
about
an
here
is
on
that

Sentence stem
Here is a _____.

Ask children to read these words:

zebra	p. 4
baboon	p. 8
rabbit	p. 16
fox	p. 17
skunk	p. 19